THE ALL-AMERICAN DOG

Man's Best Friend in Folk Art

Dr. Robert Bishop

Director,
Museum of American Folk Art

Designed by Ellen Blissman

D1449674

AVON
PUBLISHERS OF BARD, CAMELOT AND DISCUS BOOKS
In Association with
Museum of American Folk Art

THE ALL-AMERICAN DOG is an original publication of Avon Books. This work has never before appeared in book form.

Book design by Ellen Blissman.

Photography for the Museum of American Folk Art by Joshua Schreier.

AVON BOOKS
A division of
The Hearst Corporation
959 Eighth Avenue
New York, New York 10019
Copyright © 1977 by the Museum of American Folk Art
Published by arrangement with the museum.
Library of Congress Catalog Card Number: 77-84981
ISBN: 0-380-01863-2

First Avon Printing, February, 1978

AVON TRADEMARK REG. U.S. PAT. OFF. AND IN
OTHER COUNTRIES, MARCA REGISTRADA, HECHO EN
U.S.A.

Printed in the U.S.A.

CONTENTS

1. BULLDOG
A. Kline
U.S.
Late 19th century
Oil on canvas
28″ x 22″
The Newtown Bee, R. Scudder Smith

A DOG IS LOVED BY OLD AND YOUNG
HE WAGS HIS TAIL, AND NOT HIS TONGUE.

—Farmer's Almanac, 1966.

"The All-American Dog—Man's Best Friend in Folk Art" was conceived as an overview of the American folk artist's use of the image of the dog. Naive painters, carvers, sculptors, rughookers, weavers, quiltmakers, needleworkers, and metalworkers are responsible for the richness and variety of material included in this exhibition. For the most part, these self-taught artists were from small towns and farming communities where the dogs they chose to depict were not purebred. So, this exhibition is about folk dogs, generally of the "Heinz 57" variety.

These all-American dogs contrast dramatically with the purebreds that the American Kennel Club has so carefully promoted in recent years. The American Kennel Club, for the purposes of show competition, has divided the 122 breeds of dogs that it recognizes into six basic groups: Sporting Dogs, Hounds, Working Dogs, Terriers, Toys, and Non-Sporting Dogs.

The interest in purebred dogs has been evident since 1576, when *Of Englishe Dogges, the diversities, the names, the natures, and the properties,* the first book concerned exclusively with dogs, was published. The "fifthe Section of this treatise" dealt with the mongrel: "Of such dogges as keep not their Kinde, of such as are mingled out of sundry sortes not imitating the conditions of some one certain spice, because they resemble no notable shape, nor exercise any worthy property of the true perfect and gentle kind, it is not necessarye that I write any more of them, but to banishe them as unprofitable I say for any use that is commendable, except to entertaine strangers with their barcking in the day time, giving warning to them of the house, that such and such be newly come, whereupon we call them admonishing Dogges, because in that point they performe theyr office."[1]

While the Kennel Club system works for the registration and showing of purebred dogs, most people have felt little hesitation about lavishing their affections on the lovable wastrels of dogdom. Dogs have historically served their masters as hunters, workers, and, most important, as devoted companions.

Primitive man first documented his use of dogs as hunters in the Stone Age paintings on cave walls and ceilings. Some of the food for nearly every primitive culture was obtained by wild dogs that had been domesticated. These animals flushed out fowl and game for the hunter.

Hunters were especially fond of Setters because their heavy coats and furry legs made them ideal for winter forays. When, toward the end of the nineteenth century, hunting for sustenance generally became hunting for sport, Setters, Pointers, and Retrievers were the most popular breeds.

Early American Colonists treasured dogs that could hunt and often went to great effort to recover a lost or stolen animal. In fact, a standard part of the brassfounder's business in Colonial America was based on dog-oriented products that helped to identify wandering animals. John Stowe, a brassfounder on Second-street, Philadelphia, advertised in the April 30, 1752, edition of the *Pennsylvania Gazette*: "All sorts of brasses . . . brass furniture of every sort for coaches, chaises . . . best quality shoe-buckles, house spring-bells, ditto for horses . . . dog-collars, with a variety of other brass work, at the most reasonable rates."

Furthermore, early newspapers contained many advertisements placed by dog owners whose prized pets had strayed. The *Newport Mercury*, Newport, Rhode Island, for February 24–March 3, 1766, announced: "LOST, stolen, or strayed, a white and liver coloured Bitch, spotted in the Face somewhat remarkable, with a black Leather Garter about its Neck, known by the Name of Phebe, and belonging to an Officer on board his Majesty's Ship Maidstone. Whoever secures the same, and brings her to the right Owner, or to Mr. Cahoon's Coffee-House, shall receive a Dollar Reward, and no Questions asked." In 1791 the *Independent Gazeteer, (and Agricultural Repository)*, a Philadelphia newspaper, ran the following advertisement on Saturday, November 12: "A Spaniel Dog Lost, LOST, on Friday the 28th ult. A White and Brown spotted SPANIEL DOG, about 4 months old: has remarkable long ears, and his tail cut short. Whoever has found said dog, and will deliver him to the Printer hereof, shall be rewarded for their trouble."

There are many incidents in American history where dogs have played an important role. For instance, during the Battle of Germantown on October 4, 1777, George Washington's army, in a surprise maneuver, devastated the enemy outposts of the Philadelphia suburb. Washington's attack ultimately proved unsuccessful and his army was repulsed. The retreating soldiers inadvertently secured a strategic advantage when a dog belonging to General William Howe, the British commander, attached himself to them. Alexander Hamilton, the youthful aide-de-camp to Washington, wrote to General Howe explaining the situation. The note and the dog were delivered to Howe, thus giving Washington's men the opportunity of spying upon the British in their official headquarters.

Americans have frequently acknowledged the dog as man's best friend. Edward Augustus Kendall of Philadelphia recorded the following dialogue in 1808: " 'The understanding of dogs,' he [the magistrate] said, 'surpasses that of all other animals, except man and the elephant.'

" 'To what then is the superiority of dogs to be attributed?' [said Caroline].

" 'Their sensibility. This makes them susceptible of affection and capable of attachment. Nature has given them their disposition, which is improved by a constant society with man.

" 'That the qualifications of dogs,' said the apothecary, 'depend materially on their education, is evident from the extreme familiarity of the habits and manners of different individuals. They are silent or noisy, according to the company they are used to keep.

" 'Very true,' said Walwyn, 'the shepherd's dog who is all day long upon silent and solitary downs, scarcely ever barks; while ladies' lap-dogs . . . are incessantly yelping.' "[2]

Kendall's praise of the American dog was endorsed by another Philadelphia publication, *The American Shooter's Manual*, published in 1827: "Among the animals most serviceable to man, is without doubt to be ranked the dog. Without indeed the assistance of those valuable qualities possessed by the canine race, many of those beasts which are now under our dominion, and upon which we depend for many of the comforts and even necessaries of life, could never have been reclaimed from their savage state, but would have been now roaming, useless, in unfrequented wilds, or if they approached the abodes of man, would exhibit themselves only in the character of a dreaded foe.

"Generous, affectionate, and trusty, in a degree far superior to every other animal, these natural qualities appear to be conferred upon the dog, solely for the benefit of mankind; that he may be rendered by them, our agreeable companion, useful servant, and most bold and safe defender."[3]

In his 1852 publication, *The Dog*, William Youett related interesting similarities of mental capability between man and canine: "We find little mention of insanity in the domesticated animals in any of our modern authors, whether treating on agriculture, horsemanship, or veterinary medicine, and yet there are some singular and very interesting cases of aberration of intellect. The inferior animals are, to a certain extent, endowed with the same faculties as ourselves. They are even susceptible to the same moral qualities. Hatred, love, fear, hope, joy, distress, courage, timidity, jealousy, and many varied passions influence and agitate them, as they do the human being. The dog is an illustration of this—the most susceptible to every impression—approaching the nearest to man in his instincts, and in many actions that surprise the philosopher, who justly appreciates it."[4]

Enthusiasm for the dog as a suitable companion for man was also expressed in 1854 in the book, *Estelle's Stories About Dogs for Good Boys and Girls*: "The dog ranks next to the human being in the scale of intelligence. From the earliest known history of this animal, he has been the friend and companion of man; protecting his habitation, ministering to his pleasures, and attaching himself to his owner with a fidelity which none else but a human being could equal. He is the one among the lower animals whose service is voluntary, and who is susceptible of disinterested affection and gratitude. Even though we exact his services, yet he still follows us, and solicits us to allow him to be our companion and our friend."[5]

Working dogs, developed especially to serve man's pragmatic needs, have always been an important part of the species. The Collie, the Shepherd, and, in most recent years, the Doberman Pinscher, are among the most popular of the 31 breeds of working dogs recognized by the American Kennel Club.

The dog has always had a significant role in wartime. The armies of Ancient Rome used working sentinel dogs. The Gauls and the Celts increased the effectiveness of their trained dogs by studding their collars with spikes and sharp, curved blades which slashed the legs of the horses of the opposing cavalrymen. Throughout the Middle Ages dogs were frequently armored in mail and during the Swiss-Burgundian War of 1476 the Swiss dogs annihilated those of the Burgundians.

In the late nineteenth century the German army undertook the thorough training of sentry dogs and between 1885 and 1905 used Airedales as message-carriers.

Dogs were an important part of the fighting forces in World War I, for over 75,000 were used by the warring nations. Experts have estimated that the number of dogs lost in action numbered some 7,000. During this conflict the United States made no use of the war dog, but Germany boasted some 30,000.

During World War II Germany is believed to have trained over 200,000 dogs and supplied Japan with 25,000. America's Canine Corps, an official part of the Army, was made up of animals donated by private individuals that were trained by volunteer members of Dogs for Defense, Inc. Ten thousand dogs did sentry duty and beach patrol with the U. S. Coast Guard in North Africa, Italy, France, and in the Pacific Theater.

The American love of folk heroes has inspired countless humorists to depict dogs as local celebrities. Richard Chase reported in *American Folk Tales & Songs* a story that originated in Eastern Kentucky:

"Once there was a man who had a fine rabbit dog—about the best in the country, he said. He thought a lot of him. One day the dog was running a rabbit in the tall grass and ran smack into a scythe someone had left there, blade up. He was running so fast the scythe split him square in two, nose to tail.

"The man slapped him together quick, wrapped him in his shirt, and ran home. He laid him in a box by the warm stove and left him there, bandaged tight together, for three weeks.

"One morning the man heard the dog bark, so he unwound the bandages and the dog jumped out, pert and smart as ever. But—

in his excitement the man had whacked him together wrong: hind end to front end.

"Well it turned out that the dog was better than ever. He could run just as fast and twice as long. He would run on one pair of legs awhile, then on the other two. He could run frontward and backward —fast and easy either way. Both ends of him could wag, both ends could bark, both ends could catch a rabbit. Better than ever, that dog was."[6]

Dogs occur most frequently in American folk sculpture. For some reason, three-dimensional portraits of favorite pets far outnumber paintings. In part, this might be the result of the ease with which an untrained artist could obtain his materials—a block of wood and a knife were sufficient.

The dog is also shown in a wide variety of textiles. Hooked rugs, quilts, samplers, and stuffed toys record its beloved image. Rughookers, like painters, frequently patterned their designs after popular lithographs of the time. Two separate collectors, from different parts of the country, have submitted objects bearing the same picture, a hooked rug, (Fig. 2), and an oil painting on tin (Fig. 3). One of the artists reversed the layout, otherwise they are identical.

2. HOOKED RUG
   Found in California
   Early 20th century
   71″ x 35″
   Suzanne Paterson

3. PORTRAIT OF FIVE
   PUPPIES Signed JWH
   U.S.
   Dated 1910
   Oil on tin
   16″ x 24″
   Kookie Johnson

4. CARVED WOODEN PATTERN
   FOR A METAL
   WEATHERVANE
   Henry Leach (?)
   U.S.
   1871
   Wood, carved and painted
   L., approx. 36″
   Courtesy of Museum of
   International Folk Art;
   Collection of Herbert W.
   Hemphill, Jr.

5. WEATHERVANE
   Cushing and White
   Watham, Massachusetts
   Circa 1871
   Metal
   L., approx. 36″
   David Davies

Potters, of course, frequently created dogs. Their representations range all the way from an elegant blue slip-decorated stoneware jug fashioned by J. and E. Norton of Bennington, Vermont, to the humorous "Fidos" shaped by Samuel and Solomon Bell working in the Shenandoah Valley during the nineteenth century.

The number and variety of weathervanes in the shape of dogs seem endless and it is especially interesting to be able to include in this exhibition both a carved wooden pattern for a weathervane (Fig. 4) and the metal vane cast from the molds made from the pattern (Fig. 5).

The dog represented for the early American seaman an almost universal taboo. Sailors, while aboard ship, seldom mentioned dogs by name, and many were so superstitious they would never say the word "dog" while at sea. The old Norse terms *bjener* or *bjenek* for dog or *benibiter* for bonebiter were, however, allowable words, and their use was considered lucky because the Norsemen were highly successful mariners. The scrimshander, however, felt little hesitation about using the image of a dog for decorative purposes; a handsome whale's tooth in this exhibition is embellished with a playful canine.

When Alaska became the 49th state in the Union, American folk art was expanded to include Alaskan ivory and stone carvings. A fine sled dog was essential to the Eskimo way of life. Among the "Kamschatkans, the Esquimaux, the Greenlanders and other northern nations, the dog constitutes their only beast of burden: Three or four Esquimaux dogs harnessed to a sledge, weighing itself 100 pounds, will draw a man over the snow or ice at the rate of one mile in six minutes. And nine of these dogs have been known to draw 1611 pounds, one mile in nine minutes."[7]

While pet dogs were dear to the hearts of most, not everyone appreciated their winning ways. The Victorian publication, *Good Manners; A Manual of Etiquette in Good Society*, published during the late nineteenth century by Porter & Coates of Philadelphia, firmly advised: "Never take favorite dogs into a drawing-room when you make a morning call. Their feet may be dusty, or they may bark at strangers, or, being of too friendly a disposition, may take the liberty of lying on a lady's gown, or jumping upon a velvet sofa or an easy chair. Besides, your friend may have a favorite cat already established before the fire, and in that case a battle may ensue. Many persons, too, have a constitutional antipathy to dogs, and others never allow their own to be seen in the reception-rooms. For all or any of these reasons, a visitor has no right to inflict upon his friend the society of his dog as well as of himself."[8]

The enthusiasm for the dog as a companion, however, has never wavered. Both the mongrel and the purebred have increased in staggering numbers. The American Kennel Club has grown from eight employees in 1919 to an organization requiring over five hundred today. Dog food companies have proliferated. Firms specializing in the manufacture of dog-related products have mushroomed and fashionable canine beauty parlors are a common sight on city streets and in country byways. With such meticulous planning for and care of the canine population, it is easy to believe that the dog is indeed man's best friend.

"The All-American Dog—Man's Best Friend in Folk Art" shows beautifully the many wonderful ways in which the dog has been recorded by the naive artist from America's earliest beginnings to today.

Notes

1. *Of Englishe Dogges, the diversities, the names, the natures, and the properties.* (n.p., 1576). Some of the spelling has been altered to make the meaning of this quotation more easily understood.
2. Edward Augustus Kendall, *Keeper's Travels in Search of His Master* (Philadelphia: n.p., 1808), pp. 42–43.

3. *The American Shooter's Manual Comprising Such Plain and Simple Rules, as are necessary to introduce the inexperienced Into a full knowledge of all that relates to The Dog, And the correct use of the Gun; Also a description of the Game of this country, by a gentleman of Philadelphia county.* (Philadelphia: Carey, Lea & Carey, 1827), p. 37.
4. William Youett, *The Dog.* (Philadelphia: Blanchard & Lea, 1852), p. 14.
5. *Estelle's Stories About Dogs for Good Boys and Girls.* (Boston: Phillip, Sampson and Company, 1854), pp. 7–8.
6. Richard Chase, *American Folk Tales & Songs.* (n.p., n.d.), pp. 97–98.
7. *The American Shooter's Manual*, p. 62.
8. *Good Manners; A Manual of Etiquette in Good Society.* (Philadelphia: Porter & Coates, n.d.), p. 26.

PAINTING

6. PORTRAIT OF A DOG
   U.S.
   Late 19th century
   Pastel
   20" x 24"
   James M. Rickard

Newfoundland dogs are good to save children from drowning, but you must have a pond of water handy and a child, or else there will be no profit in boarding a Newfoundland.

—Josh Billings.

7. THE FLOOD
Clio D. Shively
Berlin Centre, Ohio
1887
Oil on canvas
27″ x 40″
Mr. and Mrs. Ridgely W. Cook

8. THREE CHILDREN WITH THEIR
   DOG
   Possibly Monmouth County, New Jersey
   Circa 1840
   Oil on canvas
   42″ x 35″
   The Newark Museum

9. PORTRAIT OF JOHN ADAMS
    Robert Peckham
    Massachusetts
    1822
    Oil on mahogany panel
    33″ x 23¼″
    Private Collection

10. PORTRAIT OF A DOG
   W. Elmer
   Oil on canvas
   25½″ x 32½″
   Mr. and Mrs. Peter Mansfield

11. PORTRAIT OF A DOG
   W. Elmer
   Oil on canvas
   25½″ x 32½″
   Mr. and Mrs. Peter Mansfield

12. PORTRAIT OF A DOG
   U.S.
   Second half of the 19th century
   Oil on canvas
   33″ x 25″
   Mr. and Mrs. Kenneth Hammitt

13. PORTRAIT OF MISS JONES, BOSTON
William Matthew Prior
New England
1846
Oil on canvas
30″ x 25″
Private Collection

14. ASA AND SUSANNA CAVERLY
Joseph H. Davis
New England
1836
Watercolor on paper
11″ x 14″
Davis also painted portraits of Asa's
brother, Elder John Caverly, and his wife,
Nancy; and of Captain Azariah, another
brother, and his wife, Eliza; and of his
nephews, Everett, John, and Zachariah.
Mr. and Mrs. Edwin Braman

Think of the kind-hearted dog, and let it lead you to be kind to him. Perhaps you know some animals of this race that may be cross and savage; it is then wise to withhold your caresses from them, but never use them ill. I have known kind dogs made cross by the unkindness of men and children. You do not like to be plagued, they have not sense enough always to reflect that all men or boys are not equally unkind. You, on the contrary, should learn to remember that, if some dogs are crabbed, all are not so; and you should never make all suffer for the faults of a few.

—Ingram Cobbin.

16. PORTRAIT OF TWO DOGS
    U.S.
    Second half of the 19th century
    Watercolor
    7½" x 6"
    Mr. and Mrs. Kenneth Hammitt

17. PORTRAIT OF A RECLINING DOG
    Henry Putney
    U.S.
    Second half of the 19th century
    Watercolor
    6" x 7"
    Mr. and Mrs. Kenneth Hammitt

15. PORTRAIT OF A DOG
    U.S.
    Second half of the 19th century
    Oil on canvas
    11" x 12"
    Mr. and Mrs. Kenneth Hammitt

18. "GEORGE BAINBRIDGE. TILTON.
1837. AGED 7 YEARS & 5 MONTHS.
JANY. 27TH."
Joseph H. Davis
New Hampshire
1837
Watercolor
8½" x 6⅜"
Private Collection

19. PET DOG
U.S.
Late 19th century
Pencil on paper
17¼" x 10¼"
Mr. and Mrs. Robert Hallock

PET DOG.

THE CENSURE OF A DOG IS SOMETHING NO MAN CAN STAND.

—Christopher Morley.

20. JOHN ASHLEY II
New York
Circa 1740
Oil on canvas
30" x 28"
This painting came from the Ashley
House in Sheffield, New York.
Mr. and Mrs. James O. Keene

21. BOY WITH DOG
    T. Gladding
    Albany, New York
    Circa 1819
    Oil on canvas
    50¼" x 40"
    Kennedy Galleries, Inc.

22. LITTLE GIRL WITH DOG
Southern Maine
Circa 1835
Oil on wood
23¾" x 32"
Mr. and Mrs. David Krashes

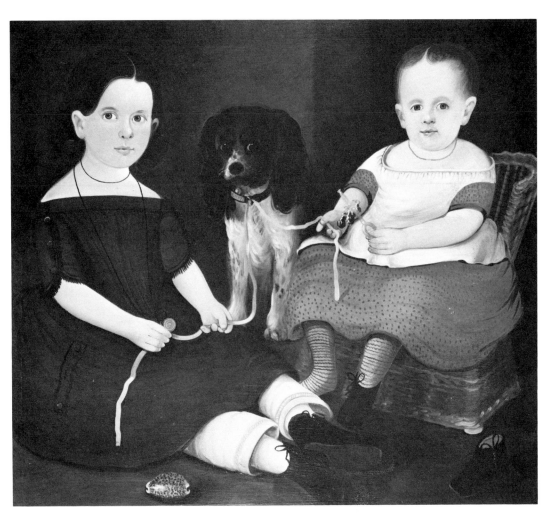

23. TWO GIRLS WITH A DOG
William Matthew Prior
New England
1840–1845
Oil on canvas
28″ x 32″
Old Sturbridge Village

24. SHEPHERD BOY
U.S.
Circa 1800
Oil on wood panel
16¾" x 11⅝"
New York State Historical Association

25. CHILD WITH POODLE AND ROSES
U.S.
Circa 1840
Oil on canvas
28¾" x 23⅝"
New York State Historical Association

26. DOG WITH RED BALL
U.S.
Late 19th century
Oil on canvas
28½″ x 22″
Mr. and Mrs. Jon Cincebox

27. PORTRAIT OF A DOG
U.S.
Circa 1840
Oil on canvas
9″ x 13″
Mr. and Mrs. Benjamin Palmer Caldwell, Jr.

28. ELIZABETHE HAAK
Jacob Maentel
Lebanon, Pennsylvania
Circa 1835
Watercolor
17½″ x 10¾″
Private Collection

29. MICHAEL HAAK
   Jacob Maentel
   Lebanon, Pennsylvania
   Circa 1835
   Watercolor
   17⅜" x 10¾"
   Private Collection

30. "THE 'POSSUM HUNT"
    Mattie Lou O'Kelley
    Georgia
    1976
    Oil on canvas
    24" x 30"
    Richard A. Miller

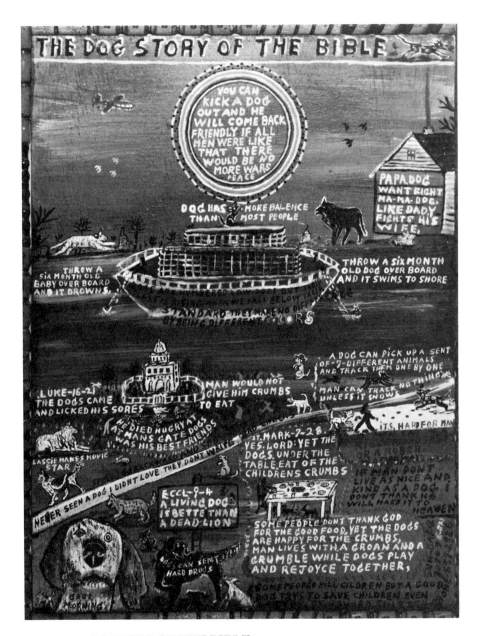

31. THE DOG STORY OF THE BIBLE
    Reverend Howard Finster
    Georgia
    1976
    Bicycle paint on wood
    18½″ x 24½″
    Chuck and Jan Rosenak

32. PORTRAIT OF ANDREW JACKSON
 TEN BROECK
 Ammi Phillips
 New York
 1834
 Oil on canvas
 39" x 34"
 Private Collection

33. LITTLE GIRL WITH DOG
School of J. Gustavus Hesselius
Pennsylvania
1735–1740
Oil on canvas
29½″ x 24½″
Chrysler Museum at Norfolk; Gift of Edgar William and Bernice Chrysler Garbisch

34. **CALLIGRAPHIC DRAWING**
     Signed and dated "Trimble, 96"
     U.S.
     Black ink on paper
     19" x 27½"
     Mr. and Mrs. Enrique Sajor

35. **"PATSY"**
     U.S.
     Second half of the 19th century
     Carved wooden wall plaque, painted
     13½" x 14"
     Mr. and Mrs. Kenneth Hammitt

THE DOGGE CALLED THE SETTER

Another sort of Dogges be there, serviceable for fowling, making no noise either with foote or with tongue, whiles they followe the game. These attend diligently ypon theyr Master and frame their conditions to such beckes, motions, and gestures, as it shall please him to exhibite and make. . . . When he hath founde the byrde, he keepeth sure and fast silence, he stayeth his steppes and wil proceede no further, and with a close, couert, watching eye, layeth his belly to the grounde and so creepeth forward like a worme.

—OF ENGLISHE DOGGES, THE DIVERSITIES, THE NAMES, THE NATURES AND THE PROPERTIES. (1576.)

36. PORTRAIT OF A DOG
Possibly Hudson Valley
1845
Oil on canvas
29½″ x 25½″
Lawrence and Halina Conklin

A REASONABLE AMOUNT O' FLEAS IS GOOD FER A DOG—
KEEPS HIM FROM BROODIN' OVER BEIN' A DOG.

—Edward Noyes Westcott.

37. MAN'S BEST FRIEND
Ohio
Circa 1860
Oil on canvas
25½″ x 32½″
Private Collection

OF THE MASTIFE OR BANDOGGE

This kinde of Dogge called a mastife or Bandogge is vaste, huge, stubborne, ougly, and eager, of a hevy and burthenous body, and therefore but of Litle swiftnesse, terrible, and frightfull to beholde, and more fearce and fell then any Arcadian curre. . . . They are serviceable against the Foxe and the Badger, to drive wilde and tame swyen out of Medowes, pastures, glebelandes and places planted with fruite, to bate and take the bull by the ear, when occasion so requireth.

—OF ENGLISHE DOGGES, THE DIVERSITIES, THE NAMES, THE NATURES AND THE PROPERTIES. (1576.)

38. FOX HUNT
U.S.
19th century
Oil on canvas
25" x 30"
Kennedy Galleries, Inc.

39. COLONIAL BOY WITH DOG
Probably Philadelphia
Last quarter of the 18th century
Oil on canvas
51" x 40½"
Mr. and Mrs. Dean Nelson

40. PORTRAIT OF JOHN
    THOMAS AVERY
    New England
    1839
    Watercolor
    19¾″ x 16″
    Mr. and Mrs. Samuel Schwartz

41. BOY WITH DOG, HORN, AND GUN
U.S.
19th century
Color pencil
21½" x 17½"
Washburn Gallery

42. "CROOK, THE AMAZING DOG"
     Larry Zingale
     U.S.
     1977
     Oil on canvas
     11″ x 14″
     Joel and Kate Kopp

SCULPTURE

43. SITTING DOG
Pennsylvania
Circa 1870
Wood, painted
H., 21"
George E. Schoellkopf, Inc.

44. FOX TERRIER
Pennsylvania
Early 20th century
Wood, carved and painted; movable joints
H., 11½"
George E. Schoellkopf, Inc.

45. STANDING DOG
Connecticut
Circa 1920
Wood, polychromed
L., 37″
Dr. and Mrs. William Greenspon

46. FOX HUNT
Justin McCarthy
U.S.
1966
Oil on board
24″ x 24″
Elias Getz

47. DALMATIAN
Attributed to J. W. Fiske
New York City
1875
Zinc
Life-size
Butch Seewagen

48. SQUIRE DONA
G. A. Hitchcock
U.S.
1894
Oil
25″ x 30″
Private Collection

49. MEMORIAL PICTURE FOR PARISH
C. ALLEN (1876–1896)
Almira Nickols
Dover, Illinois
Circa 1896
Oil on fabric
17″ x 21″
Almira Nickols was a teacher of Instrumental Music, Drawing, and Painting at the Dover (Illinois) Academy of Higher Learning. This memorial painting is a tribute to her nephew, Parish Allen, who died following the heroic rescue of his cousin from an Illinois river.
Susan Taylor Martens

50. DALMATIAN
    U.S.
    Circa 1930
    Wood, polychromed
    L., 20″
    Courtesy of Museum of International Folk
    Art; Collection of Herbert W. Hemphill, Jr.

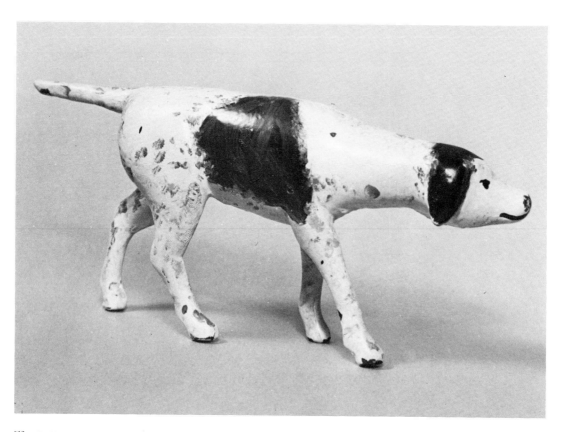

51. WHITE DOG WITH RED-BROWN
SPOTS
Alton Foundry
Lancaster, Ohio
Late 19th century
Iron, painted
L., 8¼″
Mr. and Mrs. William Gilmore

To his dog, every man is Napoleon;
HENCE THE CONSTANT POPULARITY OF DOGS.

—Aldous Huxley.

52. BEGGING DOG
Pennsylvania
Circa 1955
Wood, painted; glass eyes
H., 21½″
Herbert W. Hemphill, Jr.

53. PAIR OF DANCING DOGS
U.S.
Second half of the 19th century
Wood, painted
Mr. and Mrs. Kenneth Hammitt

LOTS OF PEOPLE HAVE A RUG.
VERY FEW HAVE A PUG.

—E. B. White.

54. PUG DOG
   U.S.
   19th century
   Pine, unpainted
   H., 4″
   Mr. and Mrs. Kenneth Hammitt

Nobody ever told Andrew he was a dog, and it's too late now. The shock of self-recognition would be too great, so it's kind of a family secret. Andrew is seven years old, but very mature for his age. He only eats people food. An ordinary garden-variety dog biscuit, even as a reward for one of his rare vocal performances for Sunday company, is regarded as an insult. Andrew prefers tacos, Big Macs, peanut butter sandwiches, chicken, fried steak, ice cubes, grapes, and okra gumbo. His favorite birthday dinner, which he anticipates as an annual event, is roast beef medium-well, smothered in Creole gravy made from flour, oil, chopped green peppers, and beef bouillon, followed by a hot fudge sundae.

Andrew doesn't know how to bark (nobody ever taught him), so he demonstrates his approval by singing. He only knows two songs, "Home on the Range" and "O Tannenbaum!," but he's working on "Across the Alley from the Alamo" and is very proud of the fact that he has already licked the first two bars and the bridge. He is in especially good voice after a refreshing bath. He bathes exclusively in Yucca Dew Shampoo, which relieves baser tensions that might otherwise lead to base desires. Andrew loves trains and Alice Faye movies on TV but hates Las Vegas.

—Rex Reed.

55. DOG SITTING ON A LOVESEAT
U.S.
1880–1900
Pine
3¾″ x 3″ x 2¼″
Herbert W. Hemphill, Jr.

56. FRONT-QUARTERS OF A DOG
U.S.
Second half of the 19th century
Wood, painted
H., 5½″
Mr. and Mrs. Kenneth Hammitt

57. SEATED SPANIEL
     U.S.
     19th century
     Chalk, mocha with smoke decoration
     H., 8½″
     Effie Thixton Arthur

58. SEATED SPANIEL
     U.S.
     19th century
     Chalk, mocha with smoke decoration
     H., 14″
     Effie Thixton Arthur

59. STANDING POODLE
    U.S.
    19th century
    Chalk, white with polychrome decoration
    H., 4½″
    Effie Thixton Arthur

60. STANDING POODLE
    U.S.
    19th century
    Chalk, white with polychrome decoration
    H., 7½″
    Effie Thixton Arthur

61. PAIR OF POODLES
Attributed to John Harrison
Bennington, Vermont
Mid-19th century
Parian
L., 8½″; H., 8¾″
Mr. and Mrs. Martin Leifer

I'll tell you why I'd rather be a dog at the White House than a President. Presidents, after their short honeymoon is over . . . they have to take a lot of abuse from everyone. Dogs, on the other hand, take no abuse from anyone, including the President.

—Traphes Bryant.

62. POODLE CARRYING A BASKET
Wilhelm Schimmel
Pennsylvania
Circa 1880
Wood, carved and painted
H., 4¾″
Mr. and Mrs. James O. Keene

63. STANDING DOG
   Bernard Langlais
   Cushing, Maine
   1975
   Wood
   L., 56″
   Ben Mildwoff

64. UMBRELLA OR CANE HANDLE IN
THE SHAPE OF A DOG-HEAD
U.S.
Late 19th century
Wood; glass eyes
L. of head, 2″
Mr. and Mrs. Lawrence Kalstone

65. CANE WITH DOG-HEAD HANDLE
Appalachia
Late 19th century
Wood; glass eyes
H. of cane, 35½″; L. of dog-head, 2¾″
The trigger mechanism under the
dog's chin opens his mouth.
Mr. and Mrs. Lawrence Kalstone

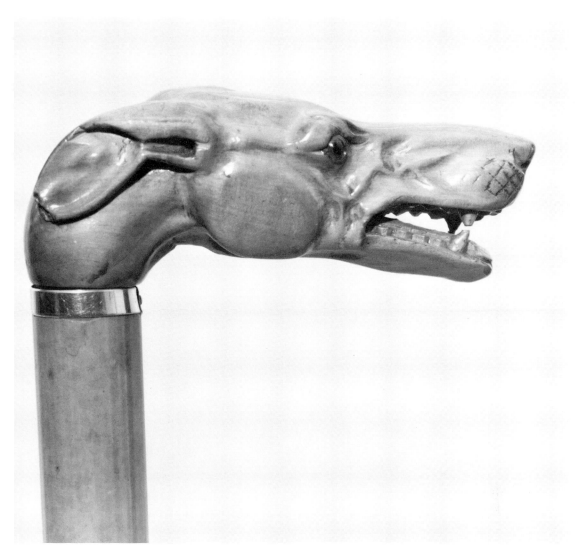

66. CANE WITH HANDLE IN THE
SHAPE OF A WHIPPET'S HEAD
New England Area
Late 19th century
Malacca; glass eyes
H. of cane, 34″; L. of dog-head, 4½″
Mr. and Mrs. Lawrence Kalstone

67. WHITE DOG WITH BLACK SPOTS
Alton Foundry
Lancaster, Ohio
Late 19th century
Iron, painted
L., 6½″
Mr. and Mrs. William Gilmore

68. DOG AND TWO PUPPIES
Morris Hirshfield
Brooklyn, New York
1944
Oil
26" x 19½"
Mr. and Mrs. Harold Ladas

69. BRIGHAM YOUNG, HIS WIFE,
AND SIX CHILDREN
William Warner Major
Utah
Circa 1847
Oil
28″ x 36″
Major, who was born in England,
joined the Church of Latter Day
Saints there in 1842 and immigrated
to America in 1844. He accompa-
nied the Mormon trek from Illinois
to Utah in 1846-48. This idealized
portrait of the Brigham Young fam-
ily was completed circa 1847.
© LDS
Church of Jesus Christ of
Latter Day Saints

70. PORTRAIT OF ELIJAH THOMPSON
U.S.
Circa 1838
Oil on tulipwood panel
30″ x 24″
Private Collection

71. "HAULING THE
    WHOLE WEEK'S
    PICKING"
    William H. Brown
    Southern U.S.
    Circa 1842
    Collage of watercolor
    and paper
    Total of 4 panels,
    19⅜" x 108³⁄₁₆"
    The Historic New
    Orleans Collection

72. MY DOG AND ME
   J. R. Adkins
   U.S.
   1965
   Oil on board
   24″ x 28″
   Elias Getz

73. PORTRAIT OF ABRAHAM LINCOLN
Malcah Zeldis
New York
20th century
Acrylic on board
23½″ x 31½″
Private Collection

74. "DOG BEAUTY PARLOR"
    Alex Maladano
    U.S.
    20th century
    Oil
    12¹¹⁄₁₆″ x 4⅝″
    Herbert W. Hemphill, Jr.

75. GRAVE MARKER
New England
1860–1880
Marble
L., 11½″
Grave markers for pets predate the
popular pet burial grounds of today.
Private Collection

76. CROUCHING DOG
Possibly carved by a Long Island decoy
maker
Early 20th century
Wood, carved and painted; glass eyes
L., 23″
David M. S. Pettigrew

77. FIGHTING PIT BULL TERRIER
Nobil Stuart
Medina, Ohio
1946
Cherry tree root; marble eyes; small nails
for eyebrows
L., 34″
The entire dog is one piece including the
tail, except for the applied ears, nails, and
teeth. Nobil Stuart passed a cherry tree
for 15 years when he suddenly realized
that he was seeing a fighting Pit Bull
Terrier in its gnarled trunk and roots. He
cut it down and carved out the dog.
Gene and Linda Kangas

78. POODLE
   Carl Wesenberg
   Michigan
   1975
   Wood, carved
   L., 9⅞″
   Jay Johnson

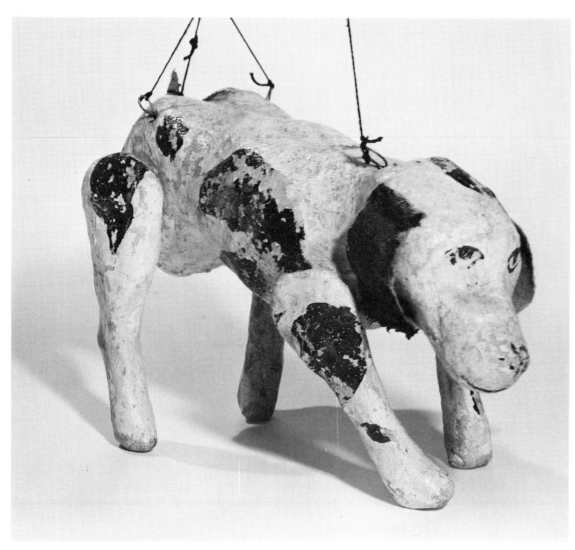

79. PUPPET
U.S.
Circa 1910
Wood
L., 7″
Kelter-Malcé Antiques

80. BOSTON BULL TERRIER
    New England
    Late 19th century
    Carved of blocked wood;
     glass eyes; metal ears
    L., 21″
    Peter F. Solana

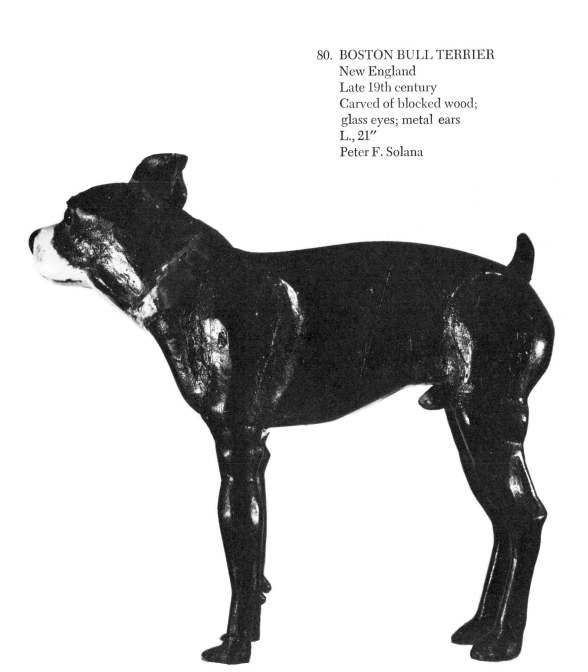

81. CLIMBING DOG
Fred Alten
Michigan
Early 20th century
Wood
H., 7¾″
Joseph and Lee Dumas

82. STANDING DOG
Fred Alten
Michigan
Early 20th century
Carved and painted wood
L., 19½″
Joseph and Lee Dumas

83. STANDING DOG
   Fred Alten
   Michigan
   Early 20th century
   Wood
   L., 10½"
   Fred Alten was born in 1872 and lived the
   first half of his life in Ohio. He moved
   to Michigan around 1912 and remained
   there until his death in 1945. An intro-
   verted man, he spent his leisure hours
   carving animals in a woodshed. Alten
   borrowed many of his ideas from a book
   entitled *Johnson's Household Book of
   Nature*, which contained descriptions and
   illustrations of modern and prehistoric
   animals based on the works of Audubon,
   Wallace, Wood, and other nineteenth-
   century naturalists.
   Joseph and Lee Dumas

84. FOX HUNT FIGURAL GROUP
   Virginia
   Early 20th century
   Carved wood, painted
   H. of horse and rider, 6"
   Mr. and Mrs. Charles V. Hagler

85. "EARL EYMAN'S DOG ACT"
   Earl Eyman
   Oklahoma
   1935
   Wood
   W., 14″
   Joel and Kate Kopp,
   America Hurrah Antiques

86. THREE-DIMENSIONAL PLAQUE
   Steven Polaha
   Reading, Pennsylvania
   1950–1960
   Wood; glass eyes
   H., 8½″
   Joel and Kate Kopp,
   America Hurrah Antiques

The superiority of Dogs over all other animals is to be attributed to their sensibility. This makes them susceptible of affection, and capable of attachment. Nature has given them this disposition, which is improved by a constant society with man. The qualifications of Dogs depend most materially upon their education as is evident from the extreme dissimilarity of the habits and manners of different individuals. They are even silent or noisy according to the company they are used to keep.

—Willis P. Hazard.

87. HUNTER WITH GUN AND DOG
U.S.
Second half of the 19th century
Wood, polychromed
H., 22¾"
This delightful carving is thought to have
been used as a trade sign.
New York State Historical Association

88. "WOMAN IN BLUE SUIT
WALKING A DOG"
Earl Eyman
Oklahoma
Circa 1935
Wood
H., 16"
Joel and Kate Kopp,
America Hurrah Antiques

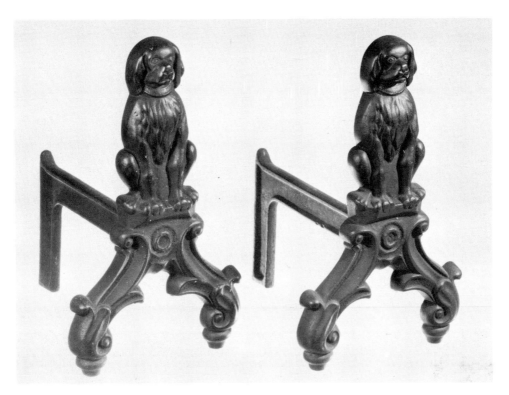

90. PAIR OF ANDIRONS
U.S.
Late 19th century
Cast iron
12″ x 7⅛″ x 10″
Greenfield Village and Henry Ford
Museum

89. SUCCESSFUL HUNTER AND HIS
DOG
S. L. Jones
West Virginia
1975
Wood
H., approx. 27″
Herbert W. Hemphill, Jr.

93. DACHSCHUND
U.S.
Early 20th century
Wood, carved
L., 16″
Private Collection

91. FIRE DOGS
Massachusetts
Hand-forged iron
L., 25″
Mr. and Mrs. Edward Abrahams

92. MINIATURE SPIT DOGS
Massachusetts
Hand-forged iron
L., 6″
Mr. and Mrs. Edward Abrahams

94. CAROUSEL DOG
Dintzel Factory
Philadelphia
1890–1910
Wood, carved
30″ x 60″
Florence and Bernard Zipkin, Mahopac
Farm and Museum

When the Kennedys came to the White House, they owned just one dog, Charlie, a welsh terrier. But gifts of dogs descended on them. The one that caused the greatest commotion was Pushinka, a present from Premier Khrushchev. Before the offspring of the Russian space dog, Strelka, could be given the run of the place, she had to be checked through security as a possible dog spy. After all, she might have been wired for sound or have an electronic "bug" implanted in her. But she didn't.

—Traphes Bryant.

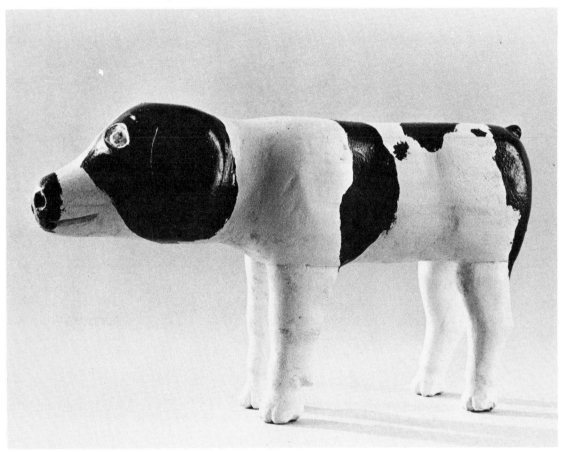

95. "WINSTON"
Edgar Tolson
Campton, Kentucky
1967
Wood, carved and painted
L. 10″
The subject of this portrait is now 15 years old and resides with his owner in Michigan.
Julie and Michael Hall

96. PIPSQUEAK
U.S.
Second half of the 19th century
Papier-mâché
5½" x 4"
This pup's mouth opens when his squeaker base is compressed.
Barbara Thornsjo, Cock Hill Farm

97. BARKING DALMATIAN
Probably New York
Early 20th century
Wood, carved
H., 6½"
Probably carved by a fireman in his spare time at the firehouse. Fire dogs were used as early as the 1870s and were most popular between 1880 and 1910, during the time of the horse-drawn steam fire engines. Dogs ran in front of the horses, alerting the citizens to clear the way for the fire engine.
Ross Becker Fire Antiques

98. PAIR OF DOGS
U.S.
19th century
Chalk, white with polychrome decoration
H., 9″
Effie Thixton Arthur

99. SEATED POODLE
U.S.
19th century
Chalk, white with polychrome decoration
H., 7″
Effie Thixton Arthur

100. SEATED POODLE
U.S.
19th century
Chalk, white with polychrome decoration
H., 6½″
Effie Thixton Arthur

101. TRADE SIGN
U.S.
Circa 1915
Plaster
33″ x 48″
Florence and Bernard Zipkin, Mahopac Farm and Museum

102. PORTRAIT OF A DOG
Felipe Archuleta
New Mexico
1975
Wood
L., 70″
H. Marc Moyens

103. CANE WITH HANDLE CARVED IN THE SHAPE OF A RUNNING DOG
Found in Connecticut
Late 19th century
Wood
H. of cane, 35″; L. of handle, 6″
Lawrence and Halina Conklin

104. POINTER WITH HANDLE IN THE SHAPE OF A DOG-HEAD
U.S.
Second half of the 19th century
Pointer, baleen; handle, ivory
L. of handle, 2¾″
Barbara Johnson Collection

105. POODLE
Found in Maine
Circa 1840
Chalk, decorated
8″ x 6¾″
Barbara Thornsjo, Cock Hill Farm

106. BOSTON BULL TERRIER
Isleboro, Maine
20th century
Wood, carved and polychromed
10½″ x 14″
Barbara Thornsjo, Cock Hill Farm

107. NUTCRACKER
Minnesota
Late 19th century
Wood, carved
8″ x 3½″
Barbara Thornsjo, Cock Hill Farm

108. SCRIMSHAW SEAL IN THE SHAPE OF A DOG-HEAD
U.S.
Second half of the 19th century
Ivory
H., 1½″
Barbara Johnson Collection

109. RUNNING DOG
U.S.
Second half of the 19th century·
Papier-mâché and composition
L., 5½″
Private Collection

110. BOSTON BULL
Found in Upstate New York
20th century
Wood
9¾″ x 10½″
Marna and Tom Anderson

111. SEATED POODLE
U.S.
19th century
Chalk, white with polychrome decoration
H., 12½″
Effie Thixton Arthur

112. CANE WITH CARVED DOG-HEAD
HANDLE
Second half of the 19th century
Wood
H. of cane, 36″; L. of dog-head, 3½″
Private Collection

113. POODLE
Aaron Mountz
Pennsylvania
Second half of the 19th century
Wood, carved
L., 24″
Private Collection

114. CANE WITH DOG-HEAD HANDLE
Massachusetts
Circa 1830
Wood with ivory handle; glass eyes
H. of cane, 33¾″; L. of dog-head, 4″
Mr. and Mrs. Lawrence Kalstone

115. INKWELL
West Virginia Area
Late 19th century
Wood; glass eyes; hinged top
L., 4¾″
Mr. and Mrs. Lawrence Kalstone

116. CANE WITH HANDLE IN THE
SHAPE OF A BULLDOG'S HEAD
New England
Circa 1850
Bamboo with ivory handle; glass eyes
H. of cane, 35″; L. of dog-head, 1¼″
Mr. and Mrs. Lawrence Kalstone

117. LETTER OPENER
West Virginia Area
Late 19th century
Wood; glass eyes
L., 14¾″
Mr. and Mrs. Lawrence Kalstone

118. DOORSTOP
S. F. Taylor
Milford, Connecticut
Late 19th century
Iron
H., 9″
Mrs. Steven Kellogg

119. SITTING DOG
Berks County, Pennsylvania
Last half of the 19th century
Wood, painted
H., 10¼″
Chris A. Machmer Antiques

120. STANDING DOG
U.S.
Late 19th century
Papier-mâché; glass eyes
L., 3″
Museum of American Folk Art;
Gift of Burton and Helaine Fendelman

121. STANDING DOG
New England
Late 19th century
Wood, unpainted
L., 6¾″
Museum of American Folk Art;
Gift of Barbara Johnson

POTTERY

122. FIGURAL GROUP
Begerly and Fleet of the Eberly Pottery
Strasburg, Virginia
1894
H., 15¼″
Private Collection

The story goes that God spoke to the new President. And God said, "I have good news and bad. The good news is that you will be permitted to bring your dog, your cat, or whatever to the White House—there is no lease restriction."

"Oh, thank you Sir," said the new President, "and what is the bad news?"

"The bad news is that the dog will be happier there than you."

—Traphes Bryant.

123. BOTTLE
Made by James A. Min
Pennsylvania
1834
Slipware
L., 9″
Inscription: "I am J. C. Neyser Doghouse Dog Art Though." The base of the bottle is decorated with pawprints.
Private Collection

125. SITTING DOG HOLDING FRUIT
BASKET IN MOUTH
Pennsylvania
Circa 1860
Glazed redware
H., 5¼″
Private Collection

124. TWO SPANIELS
John Bell
Waynesboro, Pennsylvania
Mid-19th century
Redware
H., 9″
Private Collection

126. INKWELL
     Possibly Ohio
     Second half of the 19th century
     Stoneware
     W., 8¼″
     Alice and Arthur Booth

127. WHIPPET
Solomon Bell
Winchester, Virginia
Early 19th century
Redware
L., 10″
Private Collection

128. COMBINATION BANK,
MATCHHOLDER, AND
STRIKING PLATFORM
William Hirzel
Rochester, New York
1901
Sewer-pipe pottery, a variety of
salt-glazed stoneware
H., 8″
Incised on the front, "1901," and on the
base, "William Hirzel/Rochester/NY:
1901." William Hirzel was a German im-
migrant employed as a potter at the Roch-
ester Sewer Pipe Co., Rochester, New
York.
Mr. and Mrs. George R. Hamell

129. **SEATED MINSTREL WITH DOG**
   Attributed to Samuel Bell
   Strasburg, Virginia
   Mid-19th century
   Redware
   H., 6½″
   Private Collection

130. JUG
J. & E. Norton
Bennington, Vermont
1850–1859
Stoneware with blue slip decoration
H., 15″
Mr. and Mrs. Charles V. Hagler

131. SITTING DOG
Solomon Bell
Strasburg, Virginia
Mid-19th century
Redware
H., 8½″
Private Collection

132. SITTING DOG
Pennsylvania
Circa 1860
Glazed redware
H., 5½″
Private Collection

133. **WOMAN WITH DOG**
Miles B. Carpenter
Waverly, Virginia
1971
Wood, carved and painted
H., 19″
Julie and Michael Hall

135. CROUCHING DOG
Lester and Barbara Breininger
Marked, "LBB, JM Robesonia,
Pennsylvania"
1972
Pottery
L., 5¼"
Private Collection

134. CANE WITH DALMATION HANDLE
U.S.
Second half of the 19th century
Wood
H. of cane, 33¼"; L. of dog, 4½"
Barbara Johnson Collection

136. WINGED DOG
    Steven Polaha
    Reading, Pennsylvania
    20th century
    Wood, polychromed
    L., 21½″
    Geoffrey Holder

137. GREEN-EYED DOG
    Steven Polaha
    Reading, Pennsylvania
    20th century
    Wood, polychromed
    L., 17¾″
    Geoffrey Holder

TEXTILES

138. CRIB QUILT
Pennsylvania
Circa 1910
Cotton, appliquéd and pieced
28" x 35"
Gloria List

WHY DOGS CHASE CATS

Cat and Dog decided they would store away some meat for the winter.

"I'll steal it," said Dog.

"I'll hide it," said Cat.

So Cat hid it in a hollow tree. One day when Dog wanted some, Cat ran up the tree and into the hollow, ate up the meat and tossed out the bones to Dog.

So today dogs chase cats up trees. (This story does not say whether this is in expectancy of bones or because he was once tricked out of his share of the meat.)

—Negro folktale.

139. HOOKED RUG
U.S.
Late 19th century
Wool
57″ x 29″
Jill Diesl and David Warburg

140. HOOKED RUG
     Found in Vermont
     Circa 1901
     24″ x 36″
     The skirts of the children, the dog, the
     berries, and the flower are in bas relief.
     Mr. and Mrs. Frank Pollack

141. HOOKED RUG
     Found in Western Massachusetts
     19th century
     18″ x 40″
     Willis and Karel Henry

142. HOOKED RUG
     U.S.
     1896
     27″ x 40″
     Joel and Kate Kopp,
     America Hurrah Antiques

143. HOOKED RUG
New England
Late 19th century
65″ x 37½″
Private Collection

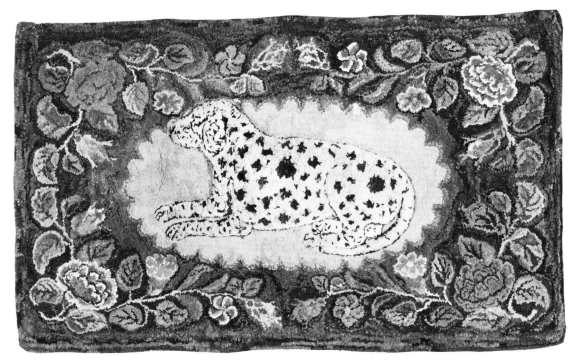

144. HOOKED RUG
 Waldoboro, Maine
 Circa 1900
 Shirred calico, patterned
 30¾″ x 52″
 Quintina Colio

145. "ROVER"
    Peekskill, New York, Area
    Second half of the 19th century
    Needlework on perforated paper
    10⅞" x 14¾"
    Mr. and Mrs. Ralph Krueger

THESE REPUBLICAN LEADERS HAVE NOT BEEN CONTENT WITH ATTACKS ON ME, ON MY WIFE, OR ON MY SONS. NO, NOT CONTENT WITH THAT, THEY NOW INCLUDE MY LITTLE DOG, FALA.

—Franklin D. Roosevelt.

146. HOOKED RUG
Pennsylvania
Last quarter of the 19th century
Cotton and wool on burlap
35½″ x 23″
Mr. and Mrs. Edward Abrahams

147. NEEDLEPOINT PILLOW TOP
      U.S.
      Circa 1880
      Wool
      8" x 12"
      Friends of Man Bookshelf

148. NEEDLEPOINT PICTURE
Wallingford, Conn., Area
Second half of the 19th century
Wool; glass eyes; shadowbox frame
12½″ x 17½″
Mr. and Mrs. Ralph Krueger

149. STUFFED DOG
U.S.
First quarter of the 20th century
Printed fabric
H., 16"
Mrs. Steven Kellogg

150. STUFFED DOG
U.S.
Possibly 20th century
H., 16″
"Hot Dog" might have been a knock-down figure at which balls were thrown.
Mrs. Steven Kellogg

151. STUFFED DOG
Amish
Ohio
Last quarter of the 19th century
H., 5¾″; L., 8¼″
Mr. and Mrs. Gary Stass

152. STUFFED PULL-TOY
U.S.
Late 19th century
Cloth; shoe-button eyes
H., 6″
Private Collection; photograph
courtesy of Kelter-Malcé Antiques

153. STUFFED DOG
Amish
Pennsylvania
1890–1920
7½″ x 7¼″
Mr. and Mrs. Robert Anderson

154. STUFFED DOG
Amish
Pennsylvania
1890–1920
16″ x 10½″
Mr. and Mrs. Robert Anderson

155. STUFFED TOY
U.S.
Late 19th century
Plush
H., 4½″
Private Collection

156. BOY WITH DOG AND RABBIT
U.S.
Second half of the 19th century
Wood, painted
H., 12″
Mr. and Mrs. Kenneth Hammitt

157. HOOKED RUG
Found in Pennsylvania
Last quarter of the 19th century
45½″ x 53″
Thomas K. Woodard,
American Antiques & Quilts

158. SAMPLER
Maria Bolen
Philadelphia
1816
20″ x 19″
Theodore Kapnek, Sr.

159. APPLIQUÉ QUILT, "GARDEN OF
     EDEN"
     Abby F. Bell Ross
     Irvington, New Jersey
     1874
     87" x 87"
     Ben Mildwoff

WEATHERVANES

160. WEATHERVANE
Possibly Cushing and White
Massachusetts
Circa 1870
Gilded copper
L., 27″
Burt Purnell

161. WEATHERVANE
Vermont
19th century
Copper
L. 35″
Barridoff Galleries

162. FOXHOUND WEATHERVANE
L. W. Cushing & Son
Waltham, Massachusetts
Circa 1883
Copper
L., 27″
Ben Mildwoff

163. POSITIVE MOLD FOR A
     SETTER WEATHERVANE
     U.S.
     Circa 1880
     Wood, carved
     Life-size
     Butch Seewagen

164. WEATHERVANE
Central Northern Maine
Circa 1920
Galvanized sheet iron with
heavier iron bracing
Overall L., 34″
Samuel Pennington

165. INDIAN AND DOG WEATHERVANE
U.S.
19th century
Sheet metal
H., 32¾″
Private Collection
(*partially illustrated on title page*)

MISCELLANEOUS

166. SCRIMSHAW TOOTH ON STAND
U.S.
1840–1860
Ivory
H., 7″
Barbara Johnson Collection

At the battle of Ballynahinch, one of the insurgents who fell in the engagement was followed by a dog. The faithful animal, for three days, lay across his master's bosom, until buried, and then for some time constantly attended his grave, [leaving] only at intervals when hunger forced him into town. His remarkable sagacity being observed, a person took him, and by care and attention, he seemed to forget the loss of his master.

      —B. F. Ells.

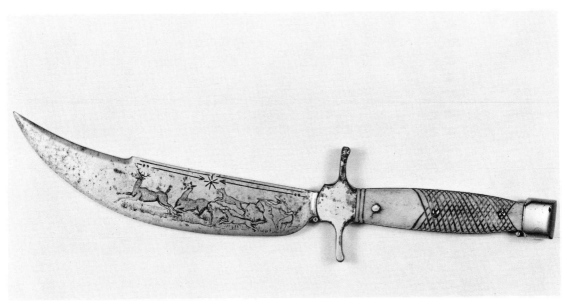

167. BUFFALO SKINNING KNIFE
Western U.S.
1870
Bone handle with white metal;
nickel-plated mounts;
hand-wrought steel blade
L., 14"
Mr. and Mrs. James O. Keene

168. FIRESCREEN
U.S.
1878
Berlin woolwork on canvas
22¼″ x 21⅜″
New Haven Colony Historical Society

AN AIREDALE, ERECT BESIDE A CHAUFFEUR OF A ROLLS-ROYCE,
OFTEN GIVES YOU THE IMPRESSION HE'S THERE BY CHOICE.

—E. B. White.

169. NINE PIN GAME PULL-TOY
   Maine
   Early 20th century
   Papier-mâché, polychrome, gesso
   L., 20″, H., 12″
   Ms. Molly Epstein

170. PIPSQUEAK
U.S.
First quarter of the 19th century
Papier-mâché, cardboard
H., 4½″; L., 3¼″
Mrs. Steven Kellogg

171. ARROWBACK WINDSOR CHILD'S
      HIGH CHAIR
     New England
     Circa 1820
     Wood
     Francis Bealey

KILLING THE DOG DOES NOT CURE THE BITE.

—Abraham Lincoln.

172. BEANBAG TARGET
Central Maine
Late 19th century
Papier-mâché
H., 16″
Barbara Thornsjo, Cock Hill Farm;
photograph courtesy of Maine Antique
Digest

In the streets of New York between 7 and 9 in the morning you will see the slow procession of dog and owner proceeding from street to tree to hydrant to trash basket. They are apartment dogs. They are taken out twice a day and, while it is a cliché, it is truly amazing how owner and dog resemble each other. They grow to walk alike, have the same set of head.

—John Steinbeck.

The dog quotations included in this book come from the following sources:

Adams, A. K. THE HOME BOOK OF HUMOROUS QUOTATIONS. New York: Dodd, Mead & Company, 1969.

Bohle, Bruce. THE HOME BOOK OF AMERICAN QUOTATIONS. New York: Dodd, Mead & Company, 1967.

Bryant, Traphes with Leighton, Frances Spatz. DOG DAYS AT THE WHITE HOUSE. New York: Macmillan Publishing Co., Inc., 1975.

Cobbin, Ingram. THE FAITHFUL DOG. New York: M. W. Dodd, 1842.

Ells, B. F. ANECDOTES OF THE DOG. Dayton, Ohio: 1853.

Fauset, Arthur Huff. TALES AND RIDDLES FROM PHILADELPHIA. Austin, Texas: "The Journal of American Folklore," Vol. 41, October-December, 1927.

Graham, Ellen. THE GROWLING GOURMET. New York: Simon & Schuster, Inc., 1976.

Hazard, Willis P. WONDERS OF THE DOG. Philadelphia: 1851.

*This exhibition was made possible in part through a generous grant
from the Wilametta Keck Day Foundation.*